"This series is a tremendous resource for those wanting to study and teach the Bible with an understanding of how the gospel is woven throughout Scripture. Here are gospel-minded pastors and scholars doing gospel business from all the Scriptures. This is a biblical and theological feast preparing God's people to apply the entire Bible to all of life with heart and mind wholly committed to Christ's priorities."

BRYAN CHAPELL, President Emeritus, Covenant Theological Seminary; Senior Pastor, Grace Presbyterian Church, Peoria, Illinois

"Mark Twain may have smiled when he wrote to a friend, 'I didn't have time to write you a short letter, so I wrote you a long letter.' But the truth of Twain's remark remains serious and universal, because well-reasoned, compact writing requires extra time and extra hard work. And this is what we have in the Crossway Bible study series *Knowing the Bible*. The skilled authors and notable editors provide the contours of each book of the Bible as well as the grand theological themes that bind them together as one Book. Here, in a 12-week format, are carefully wrought studies that will ignite the mind and the heart."

R. KENT HUGHES, Visiting Professor of Practical Theology, Westminster Theological Seminary

"*Knowing the Bible* brings together a gifted team of Bible teachers to produce a high-quality series of study guides. The coordinated focus of these materials is unique: biblical content, provocative questions, systematic theology, practical application, and the gospel story of God's grace presented all the way through Scripture."

PHILIP G. RYKEN, President, Wheaton College

"These *Knowing the Bible* volumes provide a significant and very welcome variation on the general run of inductive Bible studies. This series provides substantial instruction, as well as teaching through the very questions that are asked. *Knowing the Bible* then goes even further by showing how any given text links with the gospel, the whole Bible, and the formation of theology. I heartily endorse this orientation of individual books to the whole Bible and the gospel, and I applaud the demonstration that sound theology was not something invented later by Christians, but is right there in the pages of Scripture."

GRAEME L. GOLDSWORTHY, former lecturer, Moore Theological College; author, *According to Plan, Gospel and Kingdom, The Gospel in Revelation,* and *Gospel and Wisdom*

"What a gift to earnest, Bible-loving, Bible-searching believers! The organization and structure of the Bible study format presented through the *Knowing the Bible* series is so well conceived. Students of the Word are led to understand the content of passages through perceptive, guided questions, and they are given rich insights and application all along the way in the brief but illuminating sections that conclude each study. What potential growth in depth and breadth of understanding these studies offer! One can only pray that vast numbers of believers will discover more of God and the beauty of his Word through these rich studies."

BRUCE A. WARE, Professor of Christian Theology, The Southern Baptist Theological Seminary

KNOWING THE BIBLE

J. I. Packer, Theological Editor
Dane C. Ortlund, Series Editor
Lane T. Dennis, Executive Editor

•   •   •   •   •   •

Genesis	Psalms	Jonah, Micah, and Nahum	Ephesians
Exodus	Proverbs		Philippians
Leviticus	Ecclesiastes	Haggai, Zechariah, and Malachi	Colossians and Philemon
Numbers	Song of Solomon		
Deuteronomy	Isaiah	Matthew	1–2 Thessalonians
Joshua	Jeremiah	Mark	1–2 Timothy and Titus
Judges	Lamentations, Habakkuk, and Zephaniah	Luke	
Ruth and Esther		John	Hebrews
1–2 Samuel		Acts	James
1–2 Kings	Ezekiel	Romans	1–2 Peter and Jude
1–2 Chronicles	Daniel	1 Corinthians	1–3 John
Ezra and Nehemiah	Hosea	2 Corinthians	Revelation
Job	Joel, Amos, and Obadiah	Galatians	

•   •   •   •   •   •

J. I. PACKER is Board of Governors' Professor of Theology at Regent College (Vancouver, BC). Dr. Packer earned his DPhil at the University of Oxford. He is known and loved worldwide as the author of the best-selling book *Knowing God*, as well as many other titles on theology and the Christian life. He serves as the General Editor of the ESV Bible and as the Theological Editor for the *ESV Study Bible*.

LANE T. DENNIS is President of Crossway, a not-for-profit publishing ministry. Dr. Dennis earned his PhD from Northwestern University. He is Chair of the ESV Bible Translation Oversight Committee and Executive Editor of the *ESV Study Bible*.

DANE C. ORTLUND is Executive Vice President of Bible Publishing and Bible Publisher at Crossway. He is a graduate of Covenant Theological Seminary (MDiv, ThM) and Wheaton College (BA, PhD). Dr. Ortlund has authored several books and scholarly articles in the areas of Bible, theology, and Christian living.

DANIEL

A 12-WEEK STUDY

Todd Wilson

:: CROSSWAY®

WHEATON, ILLINOIS

Knowing the Bible: Daniel, A 12-Week Study

Copyright © 2015 by Crossway

Published by Crossway
    1300 Crescent Street
    Wheaton, Illinois 60187

Cover design: Simplicated Studio

First printing 2015

Printed in the United States of America

Trade paperback ISBN: 978-1-4335-4342-5
EPub ISBN: 978-1-4335-4345-6
PDF ISBN: 978-1-4335-4343-2
Mobipocket ISBN: 978-1-4335-4344-9

Crossway is a publishing ministry of Good News Publishers.

VP		28	27	26	25	24	23	22	21	20	19
15	14	13	12	11	10	9	8	7	6	5	4

TABLE OF CONTENTS

▲

SERIES PREFACE

KNOWING THE BIBLE, as the series title indicates, was created to help readers know and understand the meaning, the message, and the God of the Bible. Each volume in the series consists of 12 units that progressively take the reader through a clear, concise study of that book of the Bible. In this way, any given volume can fruitfully be used in a 12-week format either in group study, such as in a church-based context, or in individual study. Of course, these 12 studies could be completed in fewer or more than 12 weeks, as convenient, depending on the context in which they are used.

Each study unit gives an overview of the text at hand before digging into it with a series of questions for reflection or discussion. The unit then concludes by highlighting the gospel of grace in each passage ("Gospel Glimpses"), identifying whole-Bible themes that occur in the passage ("Whole-Bible Connections"), and pinpointing Christian doctrines that are affirmed in the passage ("Theological Soundings").

The final component to each unit is a section for reflecting on personal and practical implications from the passage at hand. The layout provides space for recording responses to the questions proposed, and we think readers need to do this to get the full benefit of the exercise. The series also includes definitions of key words. These definitions are indicated by a note number in the text and are found at the end of each chapter.

Lastly, for help in understanding the Bible in this deeper way, we urge readers to use the ESV Bible and the *ESV Study Bible*, which are available in various print and digital formats, including online editions at esv.org. The *Knowing the Bible* series is also available online.

May the Lord greatly bless your study as you seek to know him through knowing his Word.

J. I. Packer
Lane T. Dennis

WEEK 1: OVERVIEW

▲

The book of Daniel is a favorite for Sunday school teachers and students alike. And for good reason. It has all the makings of a great story—memorable characters, cliff-hanger drama, and science fiction–like visions. It's like *Harry Potter* meets *Lord of the Rings* with a dash of *Star Wars* thrown in!

Yet therein lies a potential danger. Because the human actors and events are so fascinating, we are tempted when studying this book to fix our gaze on the human plane. But when this happens we can inadvertently lose sight of the fact that this book is ultimately not about Daniel or his three friends, but about God and his victory in the world.

Sure, the book of Daniel tells Daniel's story—and a fascinating and instructive story it is. But the main purpose of Daniel is to reveal to us who God is—his character, his purposes, his way of working in the world for the good of his people. The main lesson of Daniel, then, is not, as is often assumed (and taught!), *Dare to be a Daniel!* Rather, the main point is this: *Dare to trust in Daniel's God!*

The story of Daniel is about the story of God and his victory in the world. For God is the sovereign Lord of history, the one who establishes kingdoms and brings them down. From the opening chapter and the story of Daniel's exile[1] to Babylon, to the closing chapter and its vision of the future, we see how God achieves his victory in the world. (For further background, see the *ESV Study Bible*, pages 1581–1585; available online at esv.org.)

Placing It in the Larger Story

The book of Daniel, named after and written by Daniel in the sixth century BC,[2] records the events of Daniel's life and the visions he saw from the time of his exile in 605 (1:5) until the third year of King Cyrus in 536 (10:1). Sweeping in scope, the book deals with the rise and fall of various world empires. But these historical events are seen through the lens of God's sovereign control of things, and thus serve a pastoral purpose to encourage the Jewish people during a critical time in their history. The Jews were in exile, suffering at the hand of pagan rulers who cared little for God or his people. They had every reason, then, to wonder whether God was in control, and whether he would deal with the situation—for his own glory and the good of his covenant people.

Key Verse

"I saw in the night visions, and behold, with the clouds of heaven there came one like a son of man, and he came to the Ancient of Days and was presented before him. And to him was given dominion and glory and a kingdom, that all peoples, nations, and languages should serve him; his dominion is an everlasting dominion, which shall not pass away, and his kingdom one that shall not be destroyed" (7:13–14).

Date and Historical Background

While some place the writing of Daniel in the second century BC, there is good reason to believe that Daniel himself is the author of this book and that it was composed in the sixth century BC. This was a tumultuous time in the ancient Near East and a crucial moment in the life of God's people. Daniel opens against the backdrop of the rise of the Babylonian empire, which had recently toppled the Assyrian empire. The book closes some 70 years later with the overthrow of Babylon by the Persian empire under Cyrus. It was the strategy of the Babylonians to bring to Babylon the "cream of the crop" of the peoples they conquered; the Persians reversed this process by returning the exiles to their homeland. The events of Daniel take place between these two major world-changing events: the rise of Babylon under Nebuchadnezzar and the displacement of Babylon by the Persians under Cyrus roughly 70 years later.

Outline

  I. Daniel and the Three Friends at the Babylonian Court (1:1–6:28)

    A. Prologue (1:1–21)

      1. Daniel and his friends taken into exile (1:1–7)

As You Get Started

What is your current understanding of how Daniel helps us to grasp the whole storyline of the Bible? Do you have an idea of how aspects of Daniel's message are fulfilled in the New Testament?

What is your current understanding of what Daniel contributes to Christian theology? How does his book clarify our understanding of God, Jesus Christ, sin, salvation, the end times,[3] or any other doctrine?

What aspects of the visions of Daniel have confused you? Are there any specific questions that you hope to have answered through this study?

As You Finish This Unit . . .

Take a few minutes to ask God to bless you with increased understanding and a transformed heart and life as you begin this study of Daniel.

Definitions

[1] **Exile** – Several relocations of large groups of Israelites/Jews have occurred throughout history, but "the exile" typically refers to the Babylonian exile, that is, Nebuchadnezzar's relocation of residents of the southern kingdom of Judah to Babylon in 586 BC. (Residents of the northern kingdom of Israel had been resettled by Assyria in 722 BC.) After Babylon came under Persian rule, several waves of Jewish exiles returned and repopulated Judah.

[2] **BC** – Abbreviation for "before Christ" in calendars. It immediately precedes the era designated AD (*Anno Domini*, meaning "in the year of our Lord") and, counting backwards, refers to the number of years before Jesus Christ was born.

[3] **End times** – The time associated with events prophesied in Scripture to occur at the end of the world and the second coming of Christ—also known as "the last days." Because the early church expected the return of Christ at any time, the end times can refer to any point in the period from Pentecost until Christ returns.

WEEK 2: PROLOGUE

Daniel 1:1–21

▲

This first chapter introduces the book as a whole by describing how Daniel and his three friends were deported to Babylon, where they were educated in Babylonian culture (Dan. 1:1–7). Daniel's faith is put to the test, and the chapter ends with Daniel and his three friends being promoted into the service of King Nebuchadnezzar.

The Big Picture

Daniel 1:1–21 shows us how a sovereign God accomplishes his purposes and achieves his victory by sending Daniel and his three friends into exile in Babylon.

> ### Reflection and Discussion

Read through the complete passage for this study, Daniel 1:1–21. Then review the questions below and write your notes on them concerning this introductory section to the book of Daniel. (For further background, see the *ESV Study Bible*, pages 1586–1587; available online at esv.org.)

1. Daniel and His Friends Taken into Exile (1:1–7)

The opening verse sets the stage for Nebuchadnezzar's conquest of Jerusalem (v. 1). But what comes next is a bit of a shocker: "And *the Lord gave* Jehoiakim king of Judah into his hand . . ." (v. 2). Why would Daniel ascribe ultimate responsibility for the capture of Jerusalem to the Lord? What does this teach us about Daniel's view of God? And what does this imply about human agency?

Verse 2 draws considerable attention to "the vessels of the house of God," mentioning that they were seized by Nebuchadnezzar and carried off to Babylon. Take a close look at this verse. Given all the things that could have been mentioned, why draw attention to the fate of the temple vessels? Note as well where they end up—in the house of Nebuchadnezzar's god, "the treasury of his god" (v. 2). What is the significance of this?

Why does Nebuchadnezzar go to all the trouble of deporting some of the Jews to Babylon? What strategy might he have in deporting members of "the royal family and nobility" in particular (v. 3), and then training them in the culture

12

and customs of the Babylonians (v. 4), as well as providing for them materially (v. 5)?

2. Daniel and His Friends Remain Undefiled (1:8–16)

Notice how verse 8 begins with a sharp contrast: "*But* Daniel resolved that he would not defile himself with the king's food" (v. 8). Why did Daniel believe eating the king's food or drinking his wine would defile him?

Verse 9 tells us that God gave Daniel "favor and compassion." How does the Lord's favor and compassion manifest itself in Daniel's life in these verses? What concrete evidence could we point to?

3. Daniel and His Friends Promoted and Preserved (1:17–21)

This first chapter climaxes when King Nebuchadnezzar tests Daniel and his three friends in their learning. And the text isn't bashful about telling us they pass the test with flying colors; in fact, it says they were "ten times better" than anyone else. Why, though, do you think this point is emphasized?

Verse 21 looks, at first glance, to be an incidental historical detail tacked onto the end of the story: "And Daniel was there [in the court of the King of Babylon] until the first year of King Cyrus." Who is King Cyrus? And why do you think this is mentioned? What does it say about Daniel? What does it say about God?

Read through the following three sections on *Gospel Glimpses*, *Whole-Bible Connections*, and *Theological Soundings*. Then take time to consider the *Personal Implications* these sections may have for you.

▶ Gospel Glimpses

GOD GAVE. A simple subject-verb combination is used three times in the opening chapter of Daniel: "the Lord gave . . ." (1:2), "God gave . . ." (v. 9), and "God gave . . ." (v. 17). Arguably, these three "God-gives" shape the flow of this chapter and the division of its paragraphs (vv. 1–7, 8–16, 17–21). But more important, this simple expression captures the good news about what God has done in Christ: "For God so loved the world, that *he gave* his only Son" (John 3:16). What a wonderfully succinct way to express the heart of the gospel, the meaning of grace, and the story of Scripture—*God gave!* And yet, surprisingly perhaps, we find this glorious theme right here in the opening chapter of the book of Daniel.

DEFEAT AS THE PATH TO VICTORY. We're taken aback when we read in verse 2 that the Lord is the one who ultimately gave Jerusalem into the hands of Nebuchadnezzar. In a book designed to show the victory of God, this is a counterintuitive way to begin. And yet this is the gospel story—defeat is the path to victory. Before Jesus wears the crown, he bears the cross. The Son of God, the Davidic Messiah,[1] is first the Son of Man, the suffering servant who must tread the lonely path of humility and suffering and even death. "Truly, truly, I say to you, unless a grain of wheat falls into the earth and dies, it remains alone; but if it dies, it bears much fruit" (John 12:24). So, too, this is the way of the gospel in our lives: we share in Christ's suffering, "becoming like him in his death," before we "attain the resurrection from the dead" (Phil. 3:10–11).

Whole-Bible Connections

EXILE AS COVENANTAL CURSE. We will miss the full import of the opening chapter of Daniel if we fail to see the exile of the Jews to Babylon in light of the covenant curses threatened for failing to keep the stipulations of the Sinai covenant.[2] Both Leviticus (26:14–45) and Deuteronomy (28:15–68) provide an extensive list of the curses that will come upon Israel if they fail to abide by the terms of the covenant. Note that the climactic curse of the covenant is the *exile* of the nation itself (Lev. 26:33; Deut. 28:64)—viewed as a death sentence for a capital offense (i.e., apostasy/idolatry). We are therefore to understand the dramatic events of Daniel 1 as the fulfillment of the curses threatened centuries earlier (cf. Jer. 25:1–14).

BLESSING TO THE NATIONS. The book of Daniel envisions the Jews living in exile among the nations. Jeremiah prophesied of this situation, and his counsel to the exiles was clear: "Seek the welfare of the city where I have sent you into exile, and pray to the LORD on its behalf, for in its welfare you will find your welfare" (Jer. 29:7). Even though exile is an expression of God's judgment upon the nation, the Jews are nevertheless to seek to bless the people among whom they dwell. Daniel and his friends, among others, are hauled off to Babylon, yet we see them embody this commitment to bless Babylon. The story of Daniel's life can thus be seen as a partial fulfillment of God's promise to Abraham: that his offspring would be a blessing to the nations (Gen. 12:3).

Theological Soundings

SOVEREIGNTY OF GOD.[3] The God of Daniel is sovereign over men and nations. Indeed, from the start we are confronted with the Lord's sovereignty over the events of history and human circumstances. Daniel is clear that it was the Lord who ultimately orchestrated the fall of Jerusalem (Dan. 1:2). So too we learn in chapter 1 that God works in and through the most seemingly mundane details and decisions of life: the Lord is responsible for the favorable reception Daniel receives from the chief of the eunuchs (v. 9), the nourishment the four young men receive from only a vegetable diet (v. 15), and the acquisition of knowledge and insight through their study of Babylonian culture (v. 17). There is a compatibility between divine sovereignty and human agency; these are not to be set in opposition but understood as different perspectives on the same unfolding events.

CHRIST AND CULTURE. Perhaps no book in the Old Testament presents more material for thinking about the Christian presence in the world, or what has classically been referred to as the relationship between Christ and culture. Daniel and his three friends display a readiness to engage in the culture and customs of the Babylonians, and yet this clearly has limits. Daniel does not simply accommodate to the host culture of the Babylonians. At the same time, he does show a high degree of acculturation: acquiring both learning and skill in "all literature and wisdom" of the Babylonians (v. 17). This provides a good case study for thinking about the challenge of being in the world, but not of the world (John 17:15–16).

> ## ▶ Personal Implications

Take time to reflect on the implications of Daniel 1:1–21 for your own life today. Consider what you have learned that might lead you to praise God, repent of sin, and trust in his gracious promises. Make notes below on the personal implications for your walk with the Lord of the (1) *Gospel Glimpses*, (2) *Whole-Bible Connections*, (3) *Theological Soundings*, and (4) this passage as a whole.

1. Gospel Glimpses

2. Whole-Bible Connections

3. Theological Soundings

4. Daniel 1:1–21

As You Finish This Unit . . .

Take a moment now to ask for the Lord's blessing and help as you continue in this study of Daniel. And take a moment also to look back through this unit of study, to reflect on some key things that the Lord may be teaching you—and perhaps to highlight and underline these things to review again in the future.

Definitions

[1] **Messiah** – Transliteration of a Hebrew word meaning "anointed one," the equivalent of the Greek word *Christ*. Originally applied to anyone specially designated for a particular role, such as king or priest. Jesus himself affirmed that he was the Messiah sent from God (Matt. 16:16–17).

[2] **Covenant** – A binding agreement between two parties, typically involving a formal statement of their relationship, a list of stipulations and obligations for both parties, a list of witnesses to the agreement, and a list of curses for unfaithfulness and blessings for faithfulness to the agreement. The Old Testament is more properly understood as the old covenant, meaning the agreement established between God and his people prior to the coming of Jesus Christ and the introducing of the new covenant (New Testament).

[3] **Sovereignty** – Supreme and independent power and authority. Sovereignty over all things is a distinctive attribute of God (1 Tim. 6:15–16). He directs all things in order to carry out his purposes (Rom. 8:28–29).

Week 3:
Nebuchadnezzar's
Dream of a
Great Statue

Daniel 2:1–49

▲

The Place of the Passage

This chapter provides our first dramatic look at Daniel as an interpreter of dreams, and God as a revealer of mysteries. The story is self-contained, though its themes will reappear in later chapters of the book of Daniel. Especially significant is the division of history into earthly empires represented by Nebuchadnezzar's dream of a great statue and its interpretation. It is worth noting that this chapter introduces the portion of Daniel that was originally written in Aramaic.[1] The chapter ends with Daniel and his three friends being promoted, which prepares the way for the events to follow in chapter 3.

The Big Picture

In Daniel 2:1–49, we see that God is the God of gods and Lord of kings because he is the revealer of mysteries.

> ### ▶ Reflection and Discussion

Read through the entire text for this study, Daniel 2:1–49. Then interact with the following questions and record your notes on them concerning this section of Daniel's prophecy. (For further background, see the *ESV Study Bible*, pages 1587–1591; available online at esv.org.)

1. The Dream and Nebuchadnezzar's Threat (2:1–13)

Verse 1 tells us that Nebuchadnezzar was deeply troubled by his dreams. Why do you suppose that was? In the ancient world, dreams were viewed as communication from the gods and thus thought to anticipate the future. How does understanding this shed light on Nebuchadnezzar's response?

Nebuchadnezzar called together a group of people who were trained to interpret dreams: "the magicians, the enchanters, the sorcerers, and the Chaldeans" (v. 2). What was unusual about Nebuchadnezzar's request? How did the Chaldeans respond?

2. Daniel's Response and Prayer (2:14–24)

Daniel requests an audience with Nebuchadnezzar to interpret his dream. Why, in the flow of events in this passage, is this such a bold and faith-filled thing for Daniel to do?

After God reveals the dream to Daniel, he praises God as the one "to whom belong wisdom and might" (v. 20). But he also goes on to praise God for giving him this same "wisdom and might" (v. 23). In this context, what does it mean for God to have wisdom and might and then give it to Daniel?

----

3. Daniel Interprets the Dream (2:25–45)

In what ways does Daniel ensure that God alone gets the credit for being the revealer of mysteries?

In verses 36–43 Daniel describes the content of Nebuchadnezzar's dream. The parts of the statue represent four kingdoms, beginning with the "head of gold" (v. 38), which is Nebuchadnezzar and the Babylonian empire. Compare how these four kingdoms are described. What is the significance of each of these descriptions?

Daniel sees that a stone shall strike the image, destroying it (vv. 34–35). In light of verses 44–45, what is this stone? How does this relate to what Jesus says about his own life and ministry?

----

4. Nebuchadnezzar Promotes Daniel (2:46–49)

Nebuchadnezzar is amazed at what Daniel was able to reveal to him. He falls down prostrate and pays homage. But to whom? And yet how does that relate to what Nebuchadnezzar says in verse 47?

Daniel graciously asks the king to appoint his three friends to important positions in the empire, while Daniel stays in the court of the king (v. 49). How does this prepare for the situation in chapter 3?

Read through the following three sections on *Gospel Glimpses*, *Whole-Bible Connections*, and *Theological Soundings*. Then take time to consider the *Personal Implications* these sections may have for you.

Gospel Glimpses

SEEK MERCY. When Daniel is confronted with a truly desperate situation, the prospect of death, he doesn't despair. Instead, he calls upon his three friends "to seek mercy from the God of heaven" (v. 18). This is a gospel-laced response to crisis. It's the kind of reaction Jesus invites from his followers, regardless of their circumstances or situation in life. "Ask, and it will be given to you; seek, and you will find; knock, and it will be opened to you. For everyone who asks receives, and the one who seeks finds, and to the one who knocks it will be opened" (Matt. 7:7–8). Daniel found this promise of Jesus (made centuries later) to be gloriously true. And the only right response was adoration: "To you, O God of my fathers, I give thanks and praise" (Dan. 2:23).

INCARNATION.[2] When Nebuchadnezzar confronts his wise men with an impossible request, namely, to tell him not only the interpretation, but the content of his dream, they respond in a way that exposes the limits of human wisdom: "The thing that the king asks is difficult, and no one can show it to the king except the gods, whose dwelling is not with flesh" (Dan. 2:11). An honest confession, to be sure, but one that the gospel overturns: "And the Word became flesh and dwelt among us," the opening chapter of John's Gospel declares, "and we have seen his glory, glory as of the only Son from the Father, full of grace and truth" (John 1:14).

Whole-Bible Connections

AN EVERLASTING KINGDOM.[3] When Jesus entered into public ministry, he came preaching the gospel of God, which was an announcement of the dawning of the kingdom of God in his own person and work (Mark 1:14–15). Many centuries before, Daniel got a glimpse of this good news, the coming of an everlasting kingdom (vv. 44–45). Indeed, he saw the stone the builders would reject—the stone that became the cornerstone (v. 35; Matt. 21:42). And he understood, as Jesus demonstrated, that the initiative to establish this kingdom rests, not with man, but with God (v. 44). Ultimately, this kingdom shall reach its consummation with the dawning of a new heaven and new earth (Rev. 21:1), at which point we will be able to say, "The kingdom of the world has become the kingdom of our Lord and of his Christ, and he shall reign forever and ever" (Rev. 11:15).

MYSTERY. In Daniel 2, God stands forth as the "revealer of mysteries" (v. 47). In Daniel, as well as the rest of the Bible, the word "mystery" is not intended to refer to something cryptic or clandestine; rather, it refers to what God has yet to disclose about his purposes for the world. When God reveals to Daniel the mystery of Nebuchadnezzar's dream (vv. 18–19), Daniel is thus given insight into how history is going to unfold according to God's sovereign, saving plan. The apostle Paul speaks of this mystery in several of his letters (see Rom. 11:25; Eph. 3:1–10; Col. 1:25–26). This mystery "was kept secret for long ages but has now been disclosed and through the prophetic writings has been made known to all nations, according to the command of the eternal God, to bring about the obedience of faith" (Rom. 16:25–26).

Theological Soundings

REVELATION. The Christian faith is rooted in the fact of divine revelation. Apart from God's gracious self-disclosure, there would be no Christianity. Daniel 2, then, puts its finger on an important theological truth: divine revelation, or the fact that God "reveals deep and hidden things" (v. 22). But this chapter also reminds us of the goal of revelation: doxology, or the adoration and worship of God, which we see exemplified in both Daniel's (vv. 20–23) and Nebuchadnezzar's response to God's revealing his mystery (vv. 46–47).

WISDOM. The book of Proverbs famously asserts that wisdom, or insight for right living, begins with the fear of the Lord (Prov. 1:7). Daniel 2 both illustrates and reinforces this theme. God is the one "to whom belong wisdom and might" (Dan. 2:20). And yet God gives this wisdom to those who seek it with reverent trust, as Daniel and his three friends did (vv. 18, 23). To glean such wisdom is to get to the heart of what theology is meant to be—rightly knowing who God is.

▶ Personal Implications

Take time to reflect on the implications of Daniel 2:1–49 for your own life today. Consider what you have learned that might lead you to praise God, repent of sin, and trust in his gracious promises. Make notes below on the personal implications for your walk with the Lord of the (1) *Gospel Glimpses*, (2) *Whole-Bible Connections*, (3) *Theological Soundings*, and (4) this passage as a whole.

1. Gospel Glimpses

2. Whole-Bible Connections

3. Theological Soundings

4. Daniel 2:1–49

> ### As You Finish This Unit . . .

Take a moment now to ask for the Lord's blessing and help as you continue in this study of Daniel. And take a moment also to look back through this unit of study, to reflect on key things that the Lord may be teaching you—and perhaps to highlight and underline these things to review again in the future.

Definitions

[1] **Aramaic** – A language related to Hebrew, spoken throughout much of the ancient Near East. It was the everyday language of most Israelites after their exile to Babylon, and it continued to be spoken by many Jews (including Jesus) living in Palestine during the Roman era. Portions of the books of Ezra and Daniel were written in Aramaic.

[2] **Incarnation** – Literally "(becoming) in flesh," it refers to God becoming a human being in the person of Jesus of Nazareth.

[3] **Kingdom of God** – The sovereign rule of God. At the present time, the fallen, sinful world does not belong to the kingdom of God, since it does not submit to God's rule. Instead, God's kingdom can be found in heaven and among his people (Matt. 6:9–10; Luke 17:20–21). After Christ returns, however, the kingdoms of the world will become the kingdom of God (Rev. 11:15). Then all people will, either willingly or regretfully, acknowledge his sovereignty (Phil. 2:9–11). Even the natural world will be transformed to operate in perfect harmony with God (Rom. 8:19–23).

WEEK 4:
NEBUCHADNEZZAR
BUILDS A GREAT STATUE

Daniel 3:1–30

▲

The Place of the Passage

In Daniel 3:1–30, we see the faith of Daniel's three friends put to the test. Nebuchadnezzar erects a great statue and commands all people to fall down and worship it. Daniel's friends refuse and are thrown into a fiery furnace. But God delivers them from this peril and vindicates his own power in the eyes of Nebuchadnezzar, who responds (as we saw in Daniel 2) by ascribing praise to the God of Israel and honoring Daniel's three friends.

The Big Picture

In this chapter we see God's power at work, rescuing his people from a most perilous situation, which serves to confirm that "there is no other God who is able to rescue in this way" (3:29).

> ### Reflection and Discussion

Read through the complete passage for this study, Daniel 3:1–30. Then review the questions below and write your notes on them concerning these two cycles of judgment and grace for the nations. (For further background, see the *ESV Study Bible*, pages 1591–1592; available online at esv.org.)

1. The Nations Worship Nebuchadnezzar's Statue (3:1–7)

The statue Nebuchadnezzar builds is different from the one he saw in his dreams. What is the difference? And what does this suggest about Nebuchadnezzar's view of himself and his empire?

When describing the dedication of the great statue, these verses contain some seemingly unnecessary repetition: for example, the list of officials present (vv. 2–3) or the list of musical instruments used (vv. 5, 7). What effect is created by this repetition? Is it positive, or negative? And what does it say about the people involved?

2. Shadrach, Meshach, and Abednego Preserved in the Fiery Furnace (3:8–29)

Daniel's three friends refuse to pay homage to the statue erected by Nebuchadnezzar, and are therefore to be thrown into the fiery furnace. Look closely at their response to Nebuchadnezzar in verses 16–18. How confident are they of being delivered from the fiery furnace? What other fate do they consider a possibility?

Much to his surprise, when Nebuchadnezzar looked into the fiery furnace he saw not only the three friends alive and well, but a fourth man with them, who looked "like a son of the gods" (v. 25). Who is this person? And what does his presence with the three friends, in the fiery furnace, teach us about God's relationship to his people? You may find it helpful to read Isaiah 43:2 before answering this question.

This passage is careful to describe how the three friends appeared after they came out of the fire: "The hair of their heads was not singed, their cloaks were not harmed, and no smell of fire had come upon them" (Dan. 3:27). What does this teach us about God's ability to protect and care for his people?

3. Nebuchadnezzar Promotes Shadrach, Meshach, and Abednego (3:30)

Compare the endings of Daniel 2 and 3. What common themes do you see? What larger message is this intended to convey about God's victory and the faithfulness of God's people?

Read through the following three sections on *Gospel Glimpses*, *Whole-Bible Connections*, and *Theological Soundings*. Then take time to consider the *Personal Implications* these sections may have for you.

▶ Gospel Glimpses

DELIVERANCE. This chapter provides one of the most powerful examples of deliverance in all the Bible. Yes, the faith and courage of Daniel's three friends is truly remarkable (3:17–18). But even more so is the deliverance God achieves for them, so that not a whiff of smoke can be detected on them, even after having been in the fierce heat of the fire for some time (v. 27). It is hard to imagine a more complete deliverance than that one—that is, until you come to the New Testament, and consider the fiery furnace of hell,[1] and the deliverance God accomplishes through his Son, on behalf of his people, to rescue them from "the wrath to come" (1 Thess. 1:10).

THE FOURTH IS LIKE A SON OF THE GODS. Having commissioned his people to take the gospel to the ends of the earth, Jesus assures them of his continual presence with them: "And behold, I am with you always, to the end of the age" (Matt. 28:20). The apostle Paul understood the reality of Christ's presence to sustain him in the midst of trying circumstances: "He delivered us from such a deadly peril, and he will deliver us" (2 Cor. 1:10). So, too, do Daniel's three friends, as they enjoy the manifest presence of the preincarnate Christ shielding them from an otherwise certain death in the fiery furnace. This fourth person in the furnace, whose appearance is "like a son of the gods" (Dan. 3:25), provides a wonderful glimpse into the way in which Jesus Christ, "the great shepherd of the sheep" (Heb. 13:20), walks with his people even "through the valley of the shadow of death" (Ps. 23:4).

> ## Whole-Bible Connections

IDOLATRY.[2] Daniel 3 provides a classic case of fallen humanity's tendency to worship idols. Ever since Adam and Eve inverted the creational order by heeding the words of the Serpent, rather than trusting in the provision of God (Genesis 3), humankind has had a built-in tendency to want to construct idols in the place of God. And while these have not always taken the form of statues, humanity has consistently and cleverly found ways to exchange the glory of God for "images resembling mortal man and birds and animals and creeping things" (Rom. 1:23). The Old Testament prophets combated this issue constantly (see Isaiah 40–48), as did the earliest Christians, as they took the gospel into the cultural centers of first-century paganism (see Acts 17:16–32). God promises, however, to one day rid the world, and the human heart, of false gods: "and the LORD alone will be exalted in that day" (Isa. 2:17).

PERSECUTION. The persecution of Daniel's three friends has been the experience of God's people down through the ages. Ever since God put enmity between the Serpent and the Seed of the Woman in Genesis 3, the people of God have encountered persecution from anti-God forces in the world. The antagonism between these two peoples, and the persecution that results, is a theme that runs through the pages of Scripture—and, sadly, down through the pages of human history. The earliest Christians, of course, knew of the reality of persecution at the hands of both Jews and pagans; in fact, in Galatians 4 the apostle Paul provides a fascinating redemptive-historical reading of the friction that existed between Abraham's offspring (Gal. 4:21–28). He then adds this sober postscript: "But just as at that time he who was born according to the flesh persecuted him who was born according to the Spirit, *so also it is now*" (v. 29).

> ## Theological Soundings

CHRISTOPHANY. Although God the Son did not make his dwelling among us in the flesh until the time of the incarnation, the Old Testament provides a number of suggestive anticipations of the incarnation, when a human figure suddenly appears on the scene in the service of God. Analogous to a theophany,[3] scholars call these episodes Christophanies, literally, Christ-appearings. Perhaps the most intriguing is found in Genesis 18, when the Lord appears to Abraham and talks to him (Gen. 18:1–2; see also Gen. 32:22–32). Many students of the Bible believe we have another Christophany here in Daniel 3, with the sudden appearance of this one who is like "a son of the gods" (v. 25) and rescues Daniel's three friends.

CHURCH AND STATE. The New Testament is clear that Christians should submit to authorities (Rom. 13:1), showing proper deference and respect to political officials and governmental systems (1 Pet. 2:13–17). The followers of Jesus aren't to be renegades or political rabble-rousers. And yet submission to authorities does have a limit; in this fallen world, governments can issue decrees that directly contradict the will of God. In such cases, the path of wisdom is to do as Daniel's three friends did in the face of state-sponsored idolatry, and express your conscientious objection, while at the same time being willing to embrace the consequences of such a stand. We see Peter and the other apostles taking a similarly bold yet costly stand because they were motivated by the conviction that "We must obey God rather than men" (Acts 5:29).

▶ Personal Implications

Take time to reflect on the implications of Daniel 3:1–30 for your own life today. Consider what you have learned that might lead you to praise God, repent of sin, and trust in his gracious promises. Make notes below on the personal implications for your walk with the Lord of the (1) *Gospel Glimpses*, (2) *Whole-Bible Connections*, (3) *Theological Soundings*, and (4) this passage as a whole.

1. Gospel Glimpses

2. Whole-Bible Connections

3. Theological Soundings

4. Daniel 3:1–30

▶ **As You Finish This Unit . . .**

Take a moment now to ask for the Lord's blessing and help as you continue in this study of Daniel. And take a moment also to look back through this unit of study, to reflect on some key things that the Lord may be teaching you—and perhaps to highlight and underline these things to review again in the future.

Definitions

[1] **Hell** – A place of eternal torment for those who rebel against God and refuse to repent.

[2] **Idolatry** – In the Bible, this word usually refers to the worship of a physical object. Paul's comments in Colossians 3:5, however, suggest that idolatry can include covetousness, since greed is essentially equivalent to worshiping material things.

[3] **Theophany** – An appearance of God to a human being.

WEEK 5:
NEBUCHADNEZZAR'S DREAM OF A TOPPLED TREE

Daniel 4:1–37

This passage centers upon another of Nebuchadnezzar's dreams, this time of a toppled tree. Daniel, who did not make an appearance in the previous chapter, returns to the scene as the one to interpret Nebuchadnezzar's dream. The toppling of the tree is intended to teach Nebuchadnezzar about the preeminence of the God of Israel, a lesson he learns only by being humbled (Dan. 4:33–37). This chapter can be viewed as parallel with Daniel 5, where Belshazzar is similarly confronted with his own pride, though the outcome is decidedly different.

Daniel 4:1–37 teaches that God is able to humble those who walk in pride (v. 37).

> ## Reflection and Discussion

Read through the complete passage for this study, Daniel 4:1–37. Then review the questions below and write your notes on them concerning this section of Daniel's prophecy. (For further background, see the *ESV Study Bible*, pages 1593–1595; available online at esv.org.)

1. Nebuchadnezzar's Dream and Its Interpretation (4:1–27)

Daniel 4:1–3 provides an introduction to the events recorded in this chapter. Nebuchadnezzar declares that he wants to show "the signs and wonders" that the Most High has done for him (v. 2). What specific "signs and wonders" does he have in mind? Why does he also affirm God's everlasting kingdom in this context (v. 3)?

Nebuchadnezzar's dream involves a giant tree being chopped down by "a watcher, a holy one," who came down from heaven (v. 13). But this angel,[1] or heavenly messenger, is instructed "to leave the stump of its roots in the earth" (v. 15). What is the meaning of leaving the stump?

Daniel says that Nebuchadnezzar will experience this humbling until he acknowledges that "the Most High rules the kingdom of men and gives it to whom he will" (v. 25). But what would it mean for Nebuchadnezzar to be humble? What would be the telltale signs (see v. 27)?

2. Nebuchadnezzar's Humbling (4:28–33)

Verse 29 tells us that a whole 12 months separated the initial warning Nebuchadnezzar received and the judgment against him to bring about his humbling. What does this imply about God's ways with us?

Nebuchadnezzar experiences a thorough humbling at the hand of the Lord: "He was driven from among men and ate grass like an ox, and his body was wet with the dew of heaven till his hair grew as long as eagles' feathers, and his nails were like birds' claws" (v. 33). Why is this a fitting punishment for the sin of pride?

3. Nebuchadnezzar's Exaltation (4:34–37)

What does Nebuchadnezzar mean when he says he "lifted his eyes to heaven" (v. 34)? What immediately follows as a result of his doing that?

Nebuchadnezzar experienced "still more greatness" after he was restored (v. 36). Clearly, he has learned that the humble will be exalted. But what is the main lesson he takes away from this experience (see v. 37)?

_____

_____

_____

_____

_____

_____

_____

_____

Read through the following three sections on *Gospel Glimpses*, *Whole-Bible Connections*, and *Theological Soundings*. Then take time to consider the *Personal Implications* these sections may have for you.

▶ Gospel Glimpses

DIVINE PATIENCE. We're tempted to pass over quickly the fact that Nebuchadnezzar was given a whole year before God executed his judgment upon him for his pride (v. 29). This reminds us that God is exceedingly patient with us—even in our hard-heartedness, pride, and rebellion. Sadly, we're prone to forget or even presume upon God's "forbearance and patience" (see Rom. 2:4). Yet the gospel teaches us that God is indeed "slow to anger" (Ex. 34:6), and is therefore "patient toward you, not wishing that any should perish, but that all should reach repentance" (2 Pet. 3:9).

THE HUMBLE SHALL BE EXALTED. While the main lesson we are to take away from the example of Nebuchadnezzar is that those who exalt themselves shall be humbled (Dan. 4:37), we see the reverse in his story as well: namely, that the humble shall be exalted (v. 36). This was, of course, a recurring theme in the teaching of Jesus. In fact, this is one of the great gospel paradoxes, something Jesus himself embodied so beautifully through his sacrifice and service: "For even the Son of Man came not to be served but to serve, and to give his life as a ransom for many" (Mark 10:45). The gospel now calls believers to "humble yourselves, therefore, under the mighty hand of God so that at the proper time he may exalt you" (1 Pet. 5:6). A life of humble cross-bearing will lead to a life of sharing in the glory of God at the resurrection[2] (Phil. 3:10–11)!

Whole-Bible Connections

REACHING TO HEAVEN. Nebuchadnezzar's dream of a great tree whose top "reached to heaven" (Dan. 4:11) is eerily reminiscent of another structure forged in the depths of man's pride—the Tower of Babel, which was intended to have its "top in the heavens" (Gen. 11:4). Both of these episodes reveal the insidious and self-aggrandizing nature of pride; they also clearly reveal how God reacts to such displays of self-exaltation: the Lord of heaven cuts both down to size! Interestingly, ancient Babylon is the geographic setting for both. No wonder Babylon serves in Scripture as a symbol for all that is corrupt in the world (Revelation 18).

Theological Soundings

THE PHYSICAL EFFECTS OF SIN. One of the intriguing theological issues raised by this story is the relationship between sin and our physical bodies. Is it simply coincidental that God's judgment on Nebuchadnezzar's pride would take the form of a mental breakdown, where he loses his mind, so that he's no longer able to enjoy the company of other rational human beings but has to make his home among the beasts of the field? Or is it merely incidental that when Nebuchadnezzar has "lifted [his] eyes to heaven," he finds his reason returns to him (Dan. 4:34)? In the Western world, we're tempted to operate with a mind-body dualism that severs the connection between sin and our physical bodies. But this story invites us to ponder their interconnectedness.

JUSTICE. Having been severely humbled, Nebuchadnezzar doesn't impugn God's character, or bellyache that his treatment was unjust. Rather, he confesses that "all his works are right and his ways are just" (v. 37). This is a remarkable statement coming from the lips of a man who lost not only his power and authority but also his mind, and who was not only driven out from the company of men but also was made to dwell among animals! And yet this pagan king's humble confession teaches us that God's punishment always fits, and never exceeds, the crime, regardless of how severe it may appear to our darkened minds.

Personal Implications

Take time to reflect on the implications of Daniel 4:1–37 for your own life today. Consider what you have learned that might lead you to praise God, repent of sin, and trust in his gracious promises. Make notes below on the personal implications for your walk with the Lord of the (1) *Gospel Glimpses*, (2) *Whole-Bible Connections*, (3) *Theological Soundings*, and (4) this passage as a whole.

1. Gospel Glimpses

2. Whole-Bible Connections

3. Theological Soundings

4. Daniel 4:1–37

As You Finish This Unit . . .

Take a moment now to ask for the Lord's blessing and help as you continue in this study of Daniel. And take a moment also to look back through this unit of study, to reflect on some key things that the Lord may be teaching you—and perhaps to highlight and underline these things to review again in the future.

Definitions

[1] **Angel** – A supernatural messenger of God, often sent to carry out his will or to assist human beings in carrying out his will. Though angels are more powerful than humans and often instill awe, they are not to be worshiped (Col. 2:18; Rev. 22:8–9). The Bible does, however, note various appearances of an "Angel of the Lord," apparently a physical manifestation of God himself.

[2] **Resurrection** – The impartation of new, eternal life to a dead person at the end of time (or in the case of Jesus, on the third day after his death). This new life is not a mere resuscitation of the body (as in the case of Lazarus; John 11:1–44), but a transformation of the body to an eternal state (1 Cor. 15:35–58). Both the righteous and the wicked will be resurrected, the former to eternal life and the latter to retributive judgment (John 5:29).

WEEK 6:
BELSHAZZAR'S FEAST

Daniel 5:1–31

▲

The Place of the Passage

In Daniel 5:1–31, we are introduced to Babylon's last monarch, Belshazzar, and thus brought chronologically to the end of the Babylonian empire. The chapter describes the events of a great feast hosted by Belshazzar; it's a show of royal power, bounty, and self-satisfaction. Ironically, in the midst of the feast, Belshazzar is confronted with a message of divine judgment—the writing on the wall (v. 5). And that very night, he loses his life, when the city and thus the empire is overtaken by Darius the Mede (vv. 30–31).

The Big Picture

This chapter teaches the sober truth that sometimes people can become so hardened that they're beyond the point of redemption, so that the only thing remaining for them is judgment.

> ## Reflection and Discussion

Read through Daniel 5:1–31, which will be the focus of this week's study. Following this, review the questions below and write your responses concerning this section of the book of Daniel. (For further background, see the *ESV Study Bible*, pages 1595–1597; available online at esv.org.)

1. An Idolatrous Feast (5:1–4)

Belshazzar is enjoying a lavish feast for many, many guests. He decides, however, to drink wine out of the vessels of gold and silver brought from the temple in Jerusalem (v. 2; see 1:2). Of course, it's not as if they ran out of drinking utensils and thus had to resort to drinking out of the temple vessels. So why, then, do you think Belshazzar chose to do so? What do you suppose he was trying to say with that gesture?

Although Belshazzar was not literally Nebuchadnezzar's son, the text still refers to Nebuchadnezzar as his "father" (v. 2). Why is that? What is the significance to Belshazzar, or to the message of this story, to draw a close connection between these two rulers of Babylon?

2. An Unreadable Message (5:5–9)

While Belshazzar sees the fingers of a human hand appearing and writing on the wall, he cannot read the message. Nevertheless, he is overtaken with extreme fear, so much so that "his limbs gave way" (v. 6). Why is his immediate reaction one of fear and dread? And why does it get worse, so that he is "greatly alarmed" (v. 9)?

3. A Forgotten Interpreter (5:10–12)

The queen mother enters into the chamber to tell Belshazzar of the existence of Daniel, who had become well known as a person of "light and understanding and wisdom" (v. 11). She encourages Belshazzar to consult with this Daniel, and refers to him by his Babylonian name, Belteshazzar, which probably means "O Lady [wife of the Babylonian god Bel], protect the king!" Why is the mention of his Babylonian name so ironic in this context?

4. A Message of Judgment (5:13–31)

Daniel alone is able to interpret the writing on the wall. But before he gives Belshazzar the message, he first compares him to King Nebuchadnezzar (vv. 18–23). What are the points of similarity and the points of difference between Belshazzar and Nebuchadnezzar? It may be useful to review Daniel 4 as well.

The writing on the wall is a collection of Aramaic words, "MENE, MENE, TEKEL, and PARSIN," which are measures of weight, listed in decreasing order. Presumably, the king's wise men could have read these rather basic terms. But they were evidently unable to understand their meaning and implications. If the terms are read as verbs, the meaning becomes, "Numbered, numbered, weighed, and divided," which is the meaning Daniel gives to them (5:26–27). How does Daniel then apply this message to Belshazzar? What does it mean for him, and for his kingdom?

Read through the following three sections on *Gospel Glimpses*, *Whole-Bible Connections*, and *Theological Soundings*. Then take time to consider the *Personal Implications* these sections may have for you.

Gospel Glimpses

THE CRY FROM THE CROSS. In this story, the writing on the wall is a declaration of divine condemnation. God has tolerated Belshazzar's pride and rebellion long enough; the time has come for justice to reign. As such, this story reminds our fallen world that we too, like Belshazzar, ought to see the writing on the wall. Indeed, as the apostle Paul says, "the wrath of God is revealed from heaven against all ungodliness and unrighteousness of men" (Rom. 1:18). Are we not all liable to the same fate that met Belshazzar? And yet God, in his grace and mercy, has set forth his Son to be a sin offering for us, so that instead of having to see the writing on the wall, we can hear the cry from the cross: "It is finished" (John 19:30). "For our sake he made him to be sin who knew no sin, so that in him we might become the righteousness of God" (2 Cor. 5:21).

Whole-Bible Connections

WORSHIP OF IDOLS. During the revelry and merrymaking of Belshazzar's great feast, things come to a crescendo when Belshazzar not only defiles the vessels of the temple but indeed praises "the gods of gold and silver, bronze, iron, wood, and stone" (Dan. 5:4). This is outright blasphemy[1] and open rebellion against God, the Maker of heaven and earth, who alone deserves all glory, honor, and praise. Ironically, as pride exalts a man, he is all the more willing to prostrate himself before idols. We see this pattern again and again in the Bible, as the prophets polemicize against the folly of worshiping graven images in whom there is no life (again, see Isaiah 40–48). So, too, the apostle Paul critiques the idols of Athens, declaring that these images are merely human products, "formed by the art and imagination of man" (Acts 17:29).

Theological Soundings

WILLFUL IGNORANCE. Because of sin, human beings have the ability to induce within themselves a willful ignorance of the truth, so that what should be obvious to them is nevertheless lost upon them. They're ignorant of it, not because they lack exposure to it but because they choose to deny what is plain to them. We see willful ignorance in Belshazzar, which only multiplies his guilt before the Lord. He no doubt has heard what happened to Nebuchadnezzar, how he was humbled by the God of Israel and, once restored, gave God praise (Daniel 4). But in his pride and folly, Belshazzar seems blissfully unaware of this. And yet we learn from the apostle Paul that willful ignorance operates in every fallen heart, as people suppress the knowledge of God to such an extent that they become ignorant of him—even to the point of denying his existence as they worship idols (Rom. 1:18–23).

DIVINE JUDGMENT.[2] While God is slow to anger and abounding in steadfast love, his mercy does have limits. It is indeed possible for someone to become hardened beyond the point of redemption. Hebrews warns of this as a possibility: "If we go on sinning deliberately after receiving the knowledge of the truth, there no longer remains a sacrifice for sins, but a fearful expectation of judgment, and a fury of fire that will consume the adversaries" (Heb. 10:26–27). Belshazzar experienced God's definitive judgment against his sin. But Hebrews warns that those who are privileged to know about the good news of Jesus Christ are liable to an even more severe judgment should they reject this knowledge and profane Jesus' sacrifice (v. 29).

Personal Implications

Take time to reflect on the implications of Daniel 5:1–31 for your own life today. Consider what you have learned that might lead you to praise God, repent of sin, and trust in his gracious promises. Make notes below on the personal implications for your walk with the Lord of the (1) *Gospel Glimpses*, (2) *Whole-Bible Connections*, (3) *Theological Soundings*, and (4) this passage as a whole.

1. Gospel Glimpses

2. Whole-Bible Connections

3. Theological Soundings

4. Daniel 5:1–31

▶ **As You Finish This Unit . . .**

Take a moment now to ask for the Lord's blessing and help as you continue in this study of Daniel. And take a moment also to look back through this unit of study, to reflect on some key things that the Lord may be teaching you—and perhaps to highlight and underline these things to review again in the future.

Definitions

[1] **Blasphemy** – Any speech, writing, or action that slanders God. In the Old Testament, the penalty for blasphemy was death (Lev. 24:16), and in the New Testament, Jesus states that "the one who blasphemes against the Holy Spirit will not be forgiven" (Luke 12:10).

[2] **Judgment** – Any assessment of something or someone, especially moral assessment. The Bible also speaks of a final day of judgment when Christ returns, when all those who have refused to repent will be judged (Rev. 20:12–15).

Week 7: The Lions' Den

Daniel 6:1–28

▲

The Place of the Passage

This chapter presents the famous passage of Daniel in the lions' den. This passage has much in common with Daniel 3, when Daniel's three friends are delivered out of the fiery furnace. In this case, however, it is Daniel, rather than his three friends, who is tossed into a near-death situation; and it takes place under Darius the Mede, and thus happens to Daniel much later in his life. At this point, not only is he an old man, but he has served the empire faithfully for decades. All of this serves to heighten the dramatic tension, and to sweeten the irony when Daniel is both delivered from death and made to prosper during the reign of Darius and indeed even into the reign of Cyrus the Persian (v. 28).

The Big Picture

Daniel 6:1–28 demonstrates that God, who saved Daniel from the power of the lions, can be trusted to deliver and rescue his people from the most perilous or hopeless of situations.

> ## Reflection and Discussion

Read through the complete passage for this study, Daniel 6:1–28. Then review the questions below and write your notes on them concerning this transitional section in the book of Daniel. (For further background, see the *ESV Study Bible*, pages 1597–1599; available online at esv.org.)

1. Daniel Promoted (6:1–3)

Clearly, Daniel is a responsible and faithful senior servant of the empire. In the opening verses of this chapter, what indications do we have of Daniel's trusted status?

2. The Administrators' Plot to Remove Daniel (6:4–15)

How do Daniel's faithfulness and reliability pose a challenge to the administrators in their plot against him? What do they think is their only chance of catching Daniel doing something wrong?

Reread the Gospel accounts of the trial of Jesus. How does the administrators' plot to remove Daniel resemble the Jews' strategy to see Jesus condemned to die? What motives underlie each?

The administrators hatch a plot to catch Daniel violating the king's decree. They persuade the king to issue an edict prohibiting making petitions to any god or man other than King Darius. Presumably, they knew that this would be a problem for Daniel. What does this imply about their knowledge of Daniel's life? And how is that supported by what we read of Daniel's response to the edict (see 6:10)?

----

3. Daniel Preserved in the Lions' Den (6:16–24)

Although Darius regrets the impact of his decree upon Daniel, he goes ahead with the decision to put him into the lions' den. But clearly he is not happy about having to do so. What evidence from the text shows this?

According to Daniel, why did God deliver him from the lions' den (vv. 21–23)? Is there anything surprising or perhaps unsettling to you about what Daniel says? If so, what is it? And why?

----

4. Darius Acknowledges the Power of Daniel's God (6:25–27)

From Darius's perspective, why did God deliver Daniel from the lions' den? And what does God's deliverance of Daniel reveal about who God is?

5. Daniel Preserved until the End of the Exile (6:28)

How are the events described at the close of this chapter (v. 28) similar to those of the previous chapters? Would you say preservation is a theme of the book of Daniel? If so, how would you state that theme in your own words?

The closing verse of this chapter mentions not only Darius the Mede but also Cyrus the Persian (v. 28). Why is the mention of Cyrus significant? Read 2 Chronicles 36:22–23 and Ezra 1:1–3.

Read through the following three sections on *Gospel Glimpses*, *Whole-Bible Connections*, and *Theological Soundings*. Then take time to consider the *Personal Implications* these sections may have for you.

▶ Gospel Glimpses

RESCUED FROM LIONS. The gospel delivers us not only from sin but from Satan.[1] Scripture presents the Devil in a number of forms: sometimes he is a serpent (Gen. 3:1–14), sometimes a great dragon (Rev. 12:9), and sometimes disguised as an angel of light (2 Cor. 11:14). The apostle Peter reminds us that our adversary also "prowls around like a roaring lion, seeking someone to devour" (1 Pet. 5:8). This fallen world is truly, then, a lions' den. And yet Jesus has overcome the Evil One through his death and resurrection; so, too, shall we, by faith in Christ's shed blood for us. "Who is it that overcomes the world except the one who believes that Jesus is the Son of God?" (1 John 5:5).

ENTRUSTING HIMSELF TO HIM WHO JUDGES JUSTLY. Although Daniel 6 is ultimately about God's deliverance of Daniel from the power of the lions (v. 27), we nevertheless glean much from Daniel's valiant and courageous faith. He is steadfast in prayer, knowing that it may well cost him his life (v. 10). And he is silent before his accusers, even though he knows they want to see him removed only because of their own jealousy. Tossed to the lions, Daniel is thus a type[2] of Christ, who similarly was falsely accused by those who wanted to put an end to his life. And yet, in the midst of the swirl of false charges and allegations, Jesus did not retaliate or revile in return. In fact, he uttered not a word. Instead, he "continued entrusting himself to him who judges justly" (1 Pet. 2:23). And by so doing, he accomplished salvation for us. As Peter goes on to say, "He himself bore our sins in his body on the tree, that we might die to sin and live to righteousness. By his wounds you have been healed" (v. 24).

▶ Whole-Bible Connections

ANGELS. Angels play a vital role in the purposes of God. The book of Hebrews calls angels "ministering spirits sent out to serve for the sake of those who are to inherit salvation" (Heb. 1:14). Sometimes they are deployed by God as his messengers; at other times, they are sent by him to protect his people. We have a powerful example of their protective role in this chapter, as we learn that it was an angel who "shut the lions' mouths" so that Daniel's life would be spared (Dan. 6:22). Angels played a similar role in the rescue of Lot from Sodom and Gomorrah (Genesis 19), the protection of Elisha and the Israelites from the king of Syria (2 Kings 6:17), the deliverance of Peter from prison (Acts 5:19–20), and the rescue of Paul from those who sought to take his life (Acts 27:23–25). Truly, the Lord "will command his angels concerning you to guard you in all your ways" (Ps. 91:11).

SIGNS AND WONDERS. Throughout Scripture we see God vindicate his name and advance his purposes through the use of "signs and wonders," powerful manifestations of the presence of God in the world. Darius recognizes that the deliverance of Daniel is nothing less than the working of God's "signs and wonders" (Dan. 6:27). The downtrodden Israelites were delivered from Egyptian bondage through similar means: "And the LORD brought us out of Egypt with a mighty hand and an outstretched arm, with great deeds of terror, with signs and wonders" (Deut. 26:8; see Ex. 7:3; Neh. 9:10; Jer. 32:20). So, too, does God advance the gospel in the lives of people with "signs and wonders" done by the apostles (Acts 5:12). Similar manifestations of the powerful presence of God attended the apostle Paul's ministry among Gentiles, verifying its authenticity and guaranteeing its effectiveness (see Rom. 15:17–19). Signs and wonders are God's way of bearing witness to his presence and direction in the world (Heb. 2:4).

Theological Soundings

COMMON GRACE. One of the most intriguing features of this chapter of Daniel is the reaction of King Darius to the news that Daniel has violated his edict and must be put to death. Darius is "much distressed" by the situation (Dan. 6:14), even to the point of fasting through a sleepless night (v. 18). And yet this is a pagan king, not a member of God's family. Nevertheless, his conscience[3] is burdened by what he sees taking place. We can't help, then, but see in this story clear testimony to God's common grace, his restraining of those outside of his covenant purposes, in a way that causes them to bless those who are inside of his covenant purposes. Paul experienced similar largesse when he stood trial before King Agrippa (Acts 26). Perhaps this is why he later enjoined believers to pray "for kings and all who are in high positions, that we may lead a peaceful and quiet life, godly and dignified in every way" (1 Tim. 2:2).

Personal Implications

Take time to reflect on the implications of Daniel 6:1–28 for your own life today. Consider what you have learned that might lead you to praise God, repent of sin, and trust in his gracious promises. Make notes below on the personal implications for your walk with the Lord of the (1) *Gospel Glimpses*, (2) *Whole-Bible Connections*, (3) *Theological Soundings*, and (4) this passage as a whole.

1. Gospel Glimpses

2. Whole-Bible Connections

3. Theological Soundings

4. Daniel 6:1–28

> ## As You Finish This Unit . . .

Take a moment now to ask for the Lord's blessing and help as you continue in this study of Daniel. And take a moment also to look back through this unit of study, to reflect on some key things that the Lord may be teaching you—and perhaps to highlight and underline these things to review again in the future.

Definitions

[1] **Satan** – A spiritual being whose name means "accuser." As the leader of all the demonic forces, he opposes God's rule and seeks to harm God's people and accuse them of wrongdoing. His power, however, is confined to the bounds that God has set for him, and one day he will be destroyed along with all his demons (Matt. 25:41; Rev. 20:10).

[2] **Type/typology** – A method of interpretation in which a real, historical object, place, or person is recognized as a pattern or foreshadowing (a "type") of some later object, place, or person. For example, the Bible presents Adam as a "type" of Christ (Rom. 5:14).

[3] **Conscience** – The ability to understand the rightness or wrongness of one's actions and motives. The conscience is not identical with the inner witness of the Holy Spirit, although the Holy Spirit often employs the conscience in guiding people and convicting them of sin (Rom. 2:15).

WEEK 8: THE VISION OF FOUR GREAT BEASTS

Daniel 7:1–28

▲

Daniel 7 marks a significant transition in the book. This and the subsequent chapters describe Daniel's visions of the future. Far from being mere apocalyptic[1] speculation, however, these visions are intended to encourage God's people in the midst of their exile. The overarching message of these chapters is that God is triumphantly in control of the unfolding of history, and thus has good purposes in store for his beleaguered and persecuted people. In this chapter, we are presented with Daniel's vision of four beasts (or kingdoms), and God's plan to vindicate his people and establish his everlasting kingdom (vv. 13–14).

The Big Picture

In Daniel 7:1–28, God reveals not only how the future will unfold from Daniel's perspective, but also how he will achieve his victory and establish his everlasting dominion over the kingdoms of men (vv. 13–14).

Reflection and Discussion

Read the entire text for this week's study, Daniel 7:1–28. Then review the following questions and write your notes on them concerning this section of Daniel. (For further background, see the *ESV Study Bible*, pages 1599–1602; available online at esv.org.)

1. The Four Great Beasts (7:1–8)

Note that the vision Daniel receives in this chapter takes place during the first year of Belshazzar's reign (v. 1). The events of this chapter therefore are chronologically prior to the events of chapters 5–6. Why do you think this chapter appears here, rather than earlier in the book?

Review the content of Daniel's vision in these opening verses. What is the author trying to communicate through the imagery of darkness (7:2), the blowing of four winds (v. 2), the stirring of a great sea (v. 2), and the appearance of mutant beasts out of all of this frothy chaos (vv. 3–8)? What does this teach us about history, and earthly kings and kingdoms?

Students of the book of Daniel continue to debate the identity of the four beasts mentioned in this vision. Consulting the *ESV Study Bible* would be of help. But what can we say with some assurance about these beasts?

2. The Ancient of Days Judges the Beasts (7:9–12)

Verse 9 marks a change of scene, moving from the stormy seashore setting of verses 1–8 to an altogether different setting. How would you describe this new setting? What does the juxtaposition of these two very different scenes communicate?

At the center of this scene is the Ancient of Days (v. 9). How is he described? And what is this meant to convey about his character and purposes?

3. The Coming of the Son of Man (7:13–14)

Daniel sees a figure riding on the clouds of heaven (v. 13). What does that suggest about the nature or status of this figure? Who else in the Bible rides on the clouds of heaven (see, for example, Ps. 104:3; Isa. 19:1)?

Although this figure is clearly in some sense divine, Daniel sees that he is like "a son of man" (Dan. 7:13). How might this shed light on Jesus' favorite self-designation, "Son of Man" (see, for example, Mark 2:10, 28; 8:38)?

4. The Interpretation of the Vision (7:15–27)

While (as we saw in chapter 2) many scholars have identified the four beasts with Babylon, Medo-Persia, Greece, and Rome, the larger point to be gleaned from Daniel's vision is the ongoing conflict and chaos of earthly powers, until the Ancient of Days establishes his everlasting kingdom (v. 18). How is this a hopeful message?

Describe the sequence of events that will result in the saints possessing the kingdom (see vv. 19–27). How does this compare with what we know of the unfolding of the end times from the New Testament, especially the book of Revelation (see Revelation 18–22)?

5. Daniel's Response (7:28)

Consider Daniel's response to the vision and its interpretation (see v. 28). Is that a surprising response? How might you have expected him to respond? Why do you suppose he responded as he did?

Read through the following three sections on *Gospel Glimpses,* *Whole-Bible Connections,* **and** *Theological Soundings.* **Then take time to consider the** *Personal Implications* **these sections may have for you.**

▶ Gospel Glimpses

SON OF MAN.[2] We use a number of titles to refer to Jesus: Savior,[3] Lord,[4] Messiah,[5] Son of God. Ironically, the one we use perhaps the least, Jesus used the most; it was his favorite self-designation, namely, Son of Man. Scholars have debated Jesus' use of the phrase, but evidence strongly suggests that he drew the phrase from this chapter of the book of Daniel (see vv. 13–14). As such, it is perhaps the most exalted self-designation he could have chosen, given the fact that this figure in Daniel clearly is a divine one. And yet Jesus is very careful how and when he uses this title. In Mark's Gospel, for example, the title appears 14 times, with the overwhelming majority appearing only after Peter's confession at Caesarea Philippi, when Jesus first begins to teach them that "the Son of Man must suffer many things and be rejected by the elders and the chief priests and the scribes and be killed, and after three days rise again" (Mark 8:31). In other words, the exalted figure of Daniel 7 is first the suffering servant who sheds his own blood for the sake of his people—a stunning gospel truth!

THE GIFT OF THE KINGDOM. We live in a world of godless forces, the kind of mutant beasts Daniel sees in rapid succession in his night vision (see Dan. 7:1–8). As such, the world often seems as if it is out of control; so, too, do our lives. And yet here we recall the hope-giving assurance of our gracious Savior, Jesus, when he said to his followers, "Fear not, little flock, for it is your Father's good pleasure to give you the kingdom" (Luke 12:32). This, of course, is the overwhelming message of the book of Daniel, and of this chapter in particular, namely, that God will eventually come and render judgment in favor of the saints of the Most High, and then give to them the kingdom—and it shall be forever theirs, world without end, Amen!

Whole-Bible Connections

ANTICHRIST. Many students of Daniel have taken the "little horn" who made war with the saints and prevailed over them until the coming of the Ancient of Days (Dan. 7:21–22) to refer to that figure the New Testament calls the Antichrist. Jesus himself taught that during the end times Antichrist would come (Matt. 24:15). So, too, the apostle Paul warns of his appearing (2 Thess. 2:1–10). In his first epistle, John catches us by surprise when he says, "Children, it is the last hour, and as you have heard that antichrist is coming, so now many antichrists have come" (1 John 2:18). A little later on in this same letter, he identifies the "spirit of the antichrist" as anyone who denies Jesus has come in the flesh (4:3). This serves as a poignant reminder that the battle against antichrist is waged with truth and won by perseverance in the faith.

ALL PEOPLES, NATIONS, AND LANGUAGES. When the aged apostle John peers into the very throne room of heaven, he sees the 24 elders fall down in worship of the Lamb, and hears them sing a new song, celebrating the one who was slain and who by his blood purchased people for God "from every tribe and language and people and nation" (Rev. 5:9). This fourfold phrase appears in Daniel 7, with the triumphant vision of the one "like a son of man" who is given dominion over the whole earth, so that "all peoples, nations, and languages should serve him" (v. 14). But this points us even further back to the original use of this kind of phraseology in Genesis 10, in particular, the Table of the Nations, where we are given a record of the peoples of the earth "by their clans, their languages, their lands, and their nations" (vv. 5, 20, 31). This fourfold phrase is clearly intended to be inclusive of the whole of humanity, and in turn to represent the consummation of God's global, missional purposes in redemption—gathering ransomed people from all the peoples of the earth!

Theological Soundings

DIVINE AND HUMAN. One of the more fascinating and inspiring portions of this chapter is the description of this figure who is presented to the Ancient of Days and receives the kingdom (Dan. 7:13–14). This figure is clearly divine, since no one but God rides on the clouds of heaven; but this figure, as Daniel sees him, is also clearly human as well—he is "like a son of man" (v. 13). This person is clearly subordinate in role to the Ancient of Days and yet is also given the authority of the Ancient of Days to have dominion over "all peoples, nations, and languages" (v. 14). This paradoxical interplay points us, of course, to the paradox of the incarnation itself, where we see the second person of the Godhead take on human flesh, and be "born in the likeness of men" (Phil. 2:7).

VIEW OF HISTORY. While these chapters are apocalyptic visions and thus call for caution in identifying various aspects of the vision with specific historical realities, what nevertheless does clearly emerge from this passage (and others like it in Daniel) is a particular theological interpretation of history—what is sometimes called the history of salvation.[6] Unlike that of many ancient cultures, the biblical conception of history is linear, not cyclical. It has a definite beginning and end. And while the successive unfolding of earthly empires may appear repetitious and thus pointless, the Bible clearly envisions a sovereign God who is superintending it all and who will one day eradicate evil and put the world to rights.

Personal Implications

Take time to reflect on the implications of Daniel 7:1–28 for your own life today. Consider what you have learned that might lead you to praise God, repent of sin, and trust in his gracious promises. Make notes below on the personal implications for your walk with the Lord of the (1) *Gospel Glimpses*, (2) *Whole-Bible Connections*, (3) *Theological Soundings*, and (4) this passage as a whole.

1. Gospel Glimpses

2. Whole-Bible Connections

3. Theological Soundings

4. Daniel 7:1–28

> ## As You Finish This Unit . . .

Take a moment now to ask for the Lord's blessing and help as you continue in this study of Daniel. And take a moment also to look back through this unit of study, to reflect on some key things that the Lord may be teaching you—and perhaps to highlight and underline these things to review again in the future.

Definitions

[1] **Apocalyptic** – The distinctive literary form of the book of Revelation and of chapters 7–12 of Daniel. These parts of Scripture include revelation about the future, highly symbolic imagery, and the underlying belief that God himself will one day end the world in its present form and establish his kingdom on earth. Apocalyptic is a mode of prophecy designed to encourage and support God's people through hard times.

[2] **Son of Man** – The title Jesus uses more than any other to refer to himself (e.g., Matt. 8:20; 11:19). While labeling himself this way may underscore Jesus' humanity, the phrase is most significant in relation to the figure in Daniel 7 who receives supreme authority and an everlasting kingdom from God (compare Dan. 7:13–14 with Matt. 26:64; Mark 14:62).

[3] **Savior** – One who rescues another from disaster and destruction. Jesus is the Savior of all believers, rescuing them from sin and eternal punishment (Luke 2:11).

[4] **Lord** – Someone superior in authority or status to another, similar to "master." It is a common translation for several different Hebrew titles for God in the Old Testament, and in the New Testament the term regularly refers to Jesus. When spelled in the Old Testament with small capital letters (Lord), it translates Hebrew *Yahweh* (*YHWH*), the personal name of God.

[5] **Messiah** – Transliteration of a Hebrew word meaning "anointed one," the equivalent of the Greek word Christ. Originally applied to anyone specially designated for a particular role, such as king or priest. Jesus himself affirmed that he was the Messiah sent from God (Matt. 16:16–17).

[6] **History of salvation** – God's unified plan for all of history, to accomplish the salvation of his people. He executed this salvation plan in the work of Jesus Christ on earth, by his life, crucifixion, burial, and resurrection (1 Cor. 15:3–4). The consummation of God's plan will take place when Jesus Christ comes again to establish the "new heavens and a new earth in which righteousness dwells" (2 Pet. 3:13).

WEEK 9: THE VISION OF THE RAM, THE GOAT, AND THE LITTLE HORN

Daniel 8:1–27

The Place of the Passage

Daniel 8:1–27 presents another vision of the future from Daniel's perspective. Like the preceding, this is a vision of successive earthly kingdoms, in particular, the Medo-Persian, Greek, and Hellenistic empires. Unlike earlier visions in Daniel, however, the interpretation of the vision in this chapter is more specific in its details. And although the transitions from one kingdom to the next will involve turmoil and suffering, God's people are hereby encouraged to remain strong and steadfast, confident that God is in control and will achieve his victory.

The Big Picture

This chapter encourages God's people to continue to remain faithful in the face of persecution and the rising and falling of the kingdoms of this earth.

> ## Reflection and Discussion

Read through the complete text for this study, Daniel 8:1–27. Then review the questions below and write your notes on them concerning this central text of Daniel. (For further background, see the *ESV Study Bible*, pages 1602–1605; available online at esv.org.)

1. The Vision of the Ram and the Goat (8:1–14)

Daniel sees a ram with two horns, one of which is longer than the other (v. 3). Scholars have tended to identify the ram with the Medo-Persian empire. If this is the case, what is the significance of the different horn lengths?

Next Daniel sees a male goat that comes from the west across the face of the whole earth, "without touching the ground" (v. 5). If this is referring to Alexander the Great, what is the significance of this description? Notice, however, that even this mighty beast, which becomes "exceedingly great" and "strong" (v. 8), eventually has its own horn broken into "four conspicuous horns" (v. 8). What is the significance of this imagery? Here you may want to consult the *ESV Study Bible* notes on this section.

In verses 9–14, we are told about a "little horn" who became exceedingly powerful—"even as great as the Prince of the host" (v. 11). Many scholars consider this to be a reference to Antiochus IV Epiphanes, a member of the Seleucid dynasty who reigned from 175–164 BC. According to a Jewish historical account of this period, Antiochus desecrated the temple and thus the land of

Jerusalem and persecuted the Jews severely. How does Daniel's vision in verses 9–14 depict those very trying circumstances?

----

2. The Interpretation of the Vision (8:15–26)

In this section, the angel Gabriel appears to Daniel to provide the interpretation of the vision. You will notice that Daniel is given more specific detail about the historical circumstances represented by his dream; he is told, for example, that the two horns are the kings of Media and Persia (v. 20), and that the goat is Greece (v. 21). Why do you suppose that, in this case, Daniel is given a more specific historical interpretation of his dream? What benefit might that serve?

Daniel's vision culminates with the aggressive and bold action of the little horn. We learn that this one's power will be great—"but not by his own power" (v. 24). What does that mean? We also learn that this figure will rise up against the one whom this passage calls "the Prince of princes" (v. 25). Who is that referring to? And how does this Prince of princes respond to the little horn?

----

3. Daniel's Response (8:27)

Read the closing verse of this chapter, which describes Daniel's response. Does his reaction to his vision surprise you? Why, or why not? Why do you think he responds so dramatically, being overcome with sickness for some days? And how could he be appalled by a vision he did not understand?

Read through the following three sections on *Gospel Glimpses, Whole-Bible Connections,* and *Theological Soundings.* Then take time to consider the *Personal Implications* these sections may have for you.

▶ Gospel Glimpses

BUT BY NO HUMAN HAND. "And he shall even rise up against the Prince of princes, and he shall be broken—but by no human hand" (Dan. 8:25). Daniel's vision reminds us that God's people will find deliverance from whatever forces of evil are arrayed against them—but that it won't come by any human hand. Rather, God himself, in and through the gospel, will intervene on behalf of his people: redeeming, rescuing, saving. Even in the throes of death, the gospel promises the hope of resurrection from the dead, something God alone accomplishes through the working of his sovereign and powerful Spirit (1 Cor. 15:50–55).

THE APPOINTED TIME OF THE END. Because this chapter contains more specific historical information than other chapters, we are encouraged with the fact that there is an "appointed time of the end" (Dan. 8:19). Indeed, this chapter gives quite specific time references related to the end times[1] (see v. 14), all of which serve to bolster our confidence in the truth of God's Word—that the end is coming, and indeed is even in sight. This would have been very good news to persecuted Jewish exiles in Daniel's day; so, too, would it have been to the beleaguered believers to whom the apostle John writes in the book of Revelation. They are reminded, from the lips of Jesus himself, that the end is at hand. Jesus' last words, in fact, are these: "Surely I am coming soon" (Rev. 22:20).

Whole-Bible Connections

THE CONCENTRATION OF EVIL. This chapter presents a frightful picture of the potential of human evil, especially when it is concentrated in the power of the state. This has always posed a serious threat to the people of God. Recall the Tower of Babel many centuries earlier, the success of which would have, among other things, threatened the viability and security of God's people (Genesis 11). The earliest Christians understood this well, as they lived under the power of the mighty Roman empire. Indeed, Jesus knew this all too well, as he stood before Pontius Pilate and was then turned over to be flogged and executed as a criminal against the state (see Luke 23:1–25).

Theological Soundings

THE CHAOS OF HISTORY, THE SOVEREIGNTY OF GOD.[2] One of the impressions we get from Daniel's vision of the rise and fall of empires depicts the sheer chaos and unpredictability of human history. And yet, at the same time, we are to see—in the midst of the contingencies of this same tumultuous series of events—a sovereign God who in fact causes the rising and falling of nations. Despite appearances, God is directing the course of human history, even down to the minutest of details. If we zoom in with a narrow lens, we see only chaos, but as we zoom out and view history through the wide-angle lens of God's sovereignty, we realize that history itself tells a very different, more promising story!

Personal Implications

Take time to reflect on the implications of Daniel 8:1–27 for your own life today. Consider what you have learned that might lead you to praise God, repent of sin, and trust in his gracious promises. Make notes below on the personal implications for your walk with the Lord of the (1) *Gospel Glimpses*, (2) *Whole-Bible Connections*, (3) *Theological Soundings*, and (4) this passage as a whole.

1. Gospel Glimpses

2. Whole-Bible Connections

3. Theological Soundings

4. Daniel 8:1–27

> ## As You Finish This Unit . . .

Take a moment now to ask for the Lord's blessing and help as you continue in this study of Daniel. And take a moment also to look back through this unit of study, to reflect on some key things that the Lord may be teaching you—and perhaps to highlight and underline these things to review again in the future.

Definitions

[1] **End times** – A time associated with events prophesied in Scripture to occur at the end of the world and the second coming of Christ—also known as "the last days." Because the early church expected the return of Christ at any time, the end times can refer to any point in the period from Pentecost until Christ returns.

[2] **Sovereignty** – Supreme and independent power and authority. Sovereignty over all things is a distinctive attribute of God (1 Tim. 6:15–16). He directs all things in order to carry out his purposes (Rom. 8:28–29).

Week 10: Daniel's Prayer and Its Answer

Daniel 9:1–27

▲

The Place of the Passage

Daniel 9 is a remarkable passage. From the opening verses we learn that Daniel discovers not only the reason for the exile of the Jewish people but also the number of years that must pass before their return. He gleaned this information from the prophet Jeremiah (v. 2), thus connecting this book and this chapter in particular with the whole sweep of redemptive history, from exile to return. The chapter itself consists of Daniel's prayer of penitence[1] on behalf of his people, lamenting their sins and repenting of any wrongdoing, in the hope that God will hear his pleas for mercy and respond accordingly. The angel Gabriel, God's chosen messenger, is sent as a response to Daniel's prayer, and offers a word of reassurance that the end of exile is indeed coming.

The Big Picture

In Daniel 9:1–27, we see that sin has consequences, but that the grace of God will triumph still.

> ### Reflection and Discussion

Read through the complete passage for this study, Daniel 9:1–27. Then review the questions below and record your notes and reflections on this section of Daniel's prophecy. (For further background, see the *ESV Study Bible*, pages 1605–1608; available online at esv.org.)

1. Daniel's Prayer concerning the 70 Years (9:1–19)

Daniel is motivated to pray after having read from the book of the prophet Jeremiah (v. 1–2). Read Jeremiah 25:11 and 29:10–14 within their contexts. What does Daniel realize about the Jewish people's time in exile? How does this shed light on his motivation to pray?

As part of Daniel's prayer, he says that to the Jewish people belongs "open shame" (Dan. 9:7). What does Daniel mean by that phrase? What other words and phrases does Daniel use to describe his people's sin?

In his prayer Daniel confesses that the "curse and oath that are written in the Law of Moses" have in fact been poured out on the people of Israel (v. 11). He is referring to the curses of the covenant outlined in Leviticus 26:14–45 and Deuteronomy 28:15–68. Take a moment to review those passages and compare them with Daniel's prayer. Also review Deuteronomy 30:1–10. How might this passage inform Daniel's prayer?

Daniel offers several reasons for God to hear and heed his plea for mercy. What are these reasons? And what does this teach us about how we ought to plead with God?

2. Gabriel's Answer: 70 Sevens before the Promised Redemption (9:20–27)

As in Daniel 8, so here the angel Gabriel is sent in response to Daniel's prayer. Look closely at Gabriel's initial words to Daniel (9:22–23). What does Gabriel say that ought to encourage Daniel?

Gabriel tells Daniel that "seventy weeks" have been decreed for the people of Israel before the exile is over. Students of the book of Daniel continue to discuss and debate the meaning of these "seventy weeks," with various interpretations being offered. Here you may want to consult the *ESV Study Bible*, 1607, for more information. But regardless of the precise meaning of the "seventy weeks," what is the main point of this for God's people?

What do we learn about the promised restoration of God's people from Gabriel's reply in verses 25–27? How will it come about? What phases will it involve? And what are the major events that will take place?

Read through the following three sections on *Gospel Glimpses, Whole-Bible Connections,* and *Theological Soundings*. Then take time to consider the *Personal Implications* these sections may have for you.

Gospel Glimpses

PLEAS FOR MERCY. "Jesus, Son of David, have mercy on me!" (Luke 18:38). This was the cry of a man who knew his situation was desperate yet also held out the hope that the Son of David, Jesus of Nazareth, would be merciful. Daniel finds himself in a similarly desperate situation, as he recalls the terms of God's covenant and contemplates the sin of God's people. Without a hint of trying to downplay their plight, Daniel thus confesses on behalf of his people, "we have sinned and done wrong and acted wickedly and rebelled, turning aside from your commandments and rules" (Dan. 9:5). And while he freely acknowledges that the Lord has been entirely righteous in his care for and even his punishment of Israel, Daniel still holds out the hope that God will yet be merciful to them. Thus, in his prayer he includes "pleas for mercy" (v. 3). God's disposition to show mercy to hopeless sinners comes into clearest focus in the gospel. "According to his great mercy, he has caused us to be born again to a living hope through the resurrection of Jesus Christ from the dead" (1 Pet. 1:3).

EVERLASTING RIGHTEOUSNESS.[2] The angel Gabriel promises Daniel that God himself will bring "everlasting righteousness" to his people (Dan. 9:24). Within the context of Daniel, this refers to the state of sanctity and holiness that will come about after the "seventy weeks" decreed for God's people, which will "put an end to sin" and "atone for iniquity" (v. 24). But this points us to what God has accomplished in his Son, Jesus Christ, who has brought a definitive end to sin on the cross. As the book of Hebrews reminds us, "he has appeared once for all at the end of the ages to put away sin by the sacrifice of himself" (Heb. 9:26). As such, Jesus has truly become the believer's everlasting righteousness. "And because of him you are in Christ Jesus, who became to us wisdom from God, righteousness and sanctification and redemption" (1 Cor. 1:30).

Whole-Bible Connections

REPENTANCE, RESTORATION, AND RETURN. In Daniel 9 we see that Israel will find restoration only through repentance.[3] This is a common pattern we find in the Old and New Testaments: that genuine repentance, including the confession of sin, is the prerequisite to God's restoring and renewing his people. We find this pattern outlined most clearly for us in Deuteronomy 30, where Moses tells the people of Israel what to do once the curses of the covenant come upon them. They are to call the words of the covenant to mind, and return to the Lord in humility and repentance (vv. 1–2). When this happens within the people, God promises to return them to the land, to "gather you again from all the peoples where the Lord your God has scattered you" (v. 3). Nehemiah reflects this same pattern in his prayer of confession (Nehemiah 9). And we see the apostle Peter draw on this same pattern in his sermon in Solomon's portico: "Repent therefore, and turn back," he says to the Jews, "that your sins may be blotted out, that times of refreshing may come from the presence of the Lord, and that he may send the Christ appointed for you, Jesus" (Acts 3:19–20).

Theological Soundings

GOD-CENTEREDNESS. Daniel's prayer teaches us about the character of God, in particular, what God ultimately values. Even a cursory reading of Daniel's plea reveals that this is a man praying out of a sense of deep need, even desperation. "O my God, incline your ear," he repeatedly prays (Dan. 9:18). In light of the sin of his people, he knows he doesn't have much of a leg to stand on in prayer. This is why he appeals to what God values most—the honor of his own name. Daniel thus prays in a most God-centered way, appealing to what God prizes above everything else: "Delay not, *for your own sake*, O my God, because your city and your people are called *by your name*" (v. 19).

ATONEMENT.[4] In his response to Daniel's plea for mercy, the angel Gabriel tells him that "seventy weeks" have been decreed for his people, in order to "atone for iniquity" (v. 24). Atonement is a central theological concept in the Bible, in both the Old and the New Testament. It refers to the reconciliation of a person with God, and is often associated with the offering of a sacrifice. Occasionally, the Old Testament will refer to human suffering as a means of atonement, as is implied here in Daniel 9. But ultimately, Jesus Christ made atonement for the sins of believers. His death satisfied God's just wrath against sinful humanity, just as Old Testament sacrifices symbolized substitutionary death as payment for sin.

▶ **Personal Implications**

Take time to reflect on the implications of Daniel 9:1–27 for your own life today. Consider what you have learned that might lead you to praise God, repent of sin, and trust in his gracious promises. Make notes below on the personal implications for your walk with the Lord of the (1) *Gospel Glimpses*, (2) *Whole-Bible Connections*, (3) *Theological Soundings*, and (4) this passage as a whole.

1. Gospel Glimpses

2. Whole-Bible Connections

3. Theological Soundings

....

....

....

....

....

4. Daniel 9:1–27

....

....

....

....

....

▶ As You Finish This Unit . . .

Take a moment now to ask for the Lord's blessing and help as you continue in this study of Daniel. And take a moment also to look back through this unit of study, to reflect on some key things that the Lord may be teaching you—and perhaps to highlight and underline these things to review again in the future.

Definitions

[1] **Penitence** – The condition of being repentant and sorrowful for wrongdoing.

[2] **Righteousness** – The quality of being morally right and without sin; one of God's distinctive attributes. God imputes righteousness to (justifies) those who trust in Jesus Christ; he accepts them accordingly, as he accepts Jesus himself.

[3] **Repentance** – A complete change of heart and mind regarding one's overall attitude toward God or one's own individual actions. True regeneration and conversion is always accompanied by repentance.

[4] **Atonement** – The reconciliation of a person with God, often associated with the offering of a sacrifice. Through his death and resurrection, Jesus Christ made atonement for the sins of believers. His death satisfied God's just wrath against sinful humanity, just as Old Testament sacrifices symbolized substitutionary death as payment for sin.

WEEK 11: DANIEL'S VISION OF THE FINAL CONFLICT

Daniel 10:1–12:13

The Place of the Passage

The closing three chapters of Daniel form a single vision and bring the book to a fitting climax. With Daniel's final vision, the veil is drawn back and we are given clearer insight into spiritual battles that are reflected in earthly conflicts. While Daniel 10:1–11:1 offers rather direct insight into the nature of spiritual conflict taking place in heavenly realms, Daniel 11:2–45 goes on to provide rather specific insight into future conflict among earthly kingdoms. The final chapter of the book brings resolution to the whole, by directing our attention to the promise of glory or shame, resurrection or judgment (12:1–13). What ultimately matters is not how long this shall continue, which was Daniel's question (12:6), but how one ought to live *now*—in light of the certainty of God's final triumph (12:9–13).

The Big Picture

Daniel 10:1–12:13 shows us that despite conflicts, both earthly and spiritual, God will achieve victory in the world and will vindicate his people.

▶ Reflection and Discussion

Read through Daniel 10:1–12:13, the passage for this week's study. Then review the following questions, taking notes on the final section of Daniel's prophecy. (For further background, see the *ESV Study Bible*, pages 1609–1618; available online at esv.org.)

1. A Heavenly Messenger Brings News of Heavenly Conflict (10:1–11:1)

We are told that Daniel received a vision of a "great conflict" during the third year of Cyrus king of Persia (10:1). Two years earlier, some of the Jewish exiles were allowed to return to Jerusalem. But these Jewish returnees encountered problems. Read Ezra 1–4, which recounts the situation. Assuming Daniel knew about their trouble, what might this vision of a "great conflict" be intended to show Daniel, and through him, other Jews?

Daniel is told by his angelic messenger that he had been opposed by the "prince of the kingdom of Persia" for 21 days, but was eventually helped on his way by the angel Michael (10:13). Most scholars agree that the prince referred to here is a demonic being. If this is the case, what does this reveal about the nature of the unseen world around us?

How does Daniel respond to the insight he is given into the reality of spiritual conflict? What does the angel do in response to Daniel's reaction?

2. A Detailed Vision of Future Earthly Conflicts among Nations (11:2–45)

While the historical details of this portion of Daniel are selective, they are nevertheless of so specific a nature as to lead some critical scholars to claim that this couldn't be predictive prophecy, but the writing of history which is only made to look like prophecy. Assuming that it is predictive in nature, however, what would be the point of Daniel's receiving such a detailed account of future earthly conflicts? What useful purpose might that serve?

In order to appreciate fully the prophecies in this chapter, you are encouraged to consult the *ESV Study Bible*, 1610–1617. It would be easy to get lost in the historical complexities, but that's not the purpose. What are you most intrigued by? What is new to you in all of this? What remains unclear? Where do you need to do some more study to shore up your understanding of the history here described?

3. The Promise of Resurrection to Glory or Shame (12:1–4)

Daniel is told that there will be an intensification of trouble at the end, "such as never has been since there was a nation till that time" (v. 1). It is within this context that he hears of both the promise of resurrection and the threat of "shame and everlasting contempt" (v. 2). How do the promise and threat relate to the news of a coming great tribulation?

Jesus spoke about a coming intensification of trouble for God's people. Review his teaching on this topic in the Gospels (see Matthew 24; Mark 13; Luke 21:5–36). What parallels do you see between them and what we find here in Daniel 12? And do you see ways in which the book of Daniel has informed Jesus' teaching?

4. How Long until the End? (12:5–13)

Daniel asks the angelic messenger two different questions. What are they? And why do you think these were paramount concerns for Daniel? How does the angel respond to the questions?

The angel tells Daniel that at the end of days, while the wicked will continue to act wickedly, "those who are wise shall understand" (v. 10). What does it mean to be wise in this context? And what understanding will the wise have that the wicked will lack?

Consider the closing verse of this chapter, indeed, of the entire book of Daniel: "But go your way till the end. And you shall rest and shall stand in your allotted place at the end of the days" (v. 13). What is the angel telling Daniel to do in practical terms? And is this the sort of closing comment you would have expected for this book? What might it have meant for the first readers of Daniel's message? What should it mean for us?

Read through the following three sections on *Gospel Glimpses*, *Whole-Bible Connections*, and *Theological Soundings*. Then take time to consider the *Personal Implications* these sections may have for you.

Gospel Glimpses

NAMES WRITTEN IN THE BOOK. The angelic messenger assures Daniel that, despite the intensification of suffering near the end of history, those whose names are "found written in the book" shall be delivered (12:1). Not only here, but throughout the Bible, both Old and New Testaments, we see that God is a bookkeeper; he has written names in what is called the "book of life" (Rev. 3:5; 17:8; 20:12, 15). At the end of the book of Revelation this book is referred to as "the Lamb's book of life" (21:27), underscoring the fact that it is only because of the sacrifice of the Lamb that anyone's name is written in this book. This is a powerful image emphasizing that God "knows those who are his" (2 Tim. 2:19), and indeed that he has chosen and predestined[1] them "before the foundation of the world" (Eph. 1:4). Because God's choice is sure, our salvation is as well. This is the assurance Daniel receives in this passage, but it is also the glorious truth made possible by the gospel. Therefore, as Jesus reminds his disciples, "Rejoice that your names are written in heaven" (Luke 10:20).

▶ Whole-Bible Connections

GREAT TRIBULATION. The visions of Daniel, especially in chapters 11–12, indicate that evil will intensify toward the end of history, and that God's people will therefore have to endure a severe time of testing. "And there shall be a time of trouble," the angel says to Daniel, "such as never has been since there was a nation till that time" (12:2). Jesus, perhaps drawing on this teaching in Daniel, envisions a similar intensification of things in the last days: "For in those days there will be such tribulation as has not been from the beginning of the creation that God created until now, and never will be" (Mark 13:19; see Matt. 24:21). John may refer to this intense period of trial and suffering when he sees the dragon enraged and making war on the people of God (Rev. 12:17). Understandably, this period of history has been referred to as the "great tribulation." But regardless of when it comes, or what exactly it will be like, the message for God's people is the same, whether from Daniel or Jesus: "But the one who endures to the end will be saved" (Mark 13:13).

▶ Theological Soundings

SPIRITUAL WARFARE. Daniel refers to the conflict among earthly kingdoms, but what we learn is that this is reflective of a greater spiritual conflict taking place in heavenly realms. The New Testament supports this perspective. No small part of Jesus' ministry was taken up with conflict with spiritual forces, in particular, demons[2] (see, for example, Mark 1:21–28). And we remember what the apostle Paul says: "For we do not wrestle against flesh and blood, but against the rulers, against the authorities, against the cosmic powers over this present darkness, against the spiritual forces of evil in the heavenly places" (Eph. 6:12). Satan and his minions exercise significant influence over this "present evil age" (Gal. 1:4); Satan is, after all, the "god of this world" (2 Cor. 4:4). Yet through the cross of Christ, God has effectively disarmed these spiritual forces arrayed against the church (Col. 2:15). Furthermore, we know from both Daniel and the rest of Scripture that their ultimate judgment is sure.

DOUBLE RESURRECTION. Daniel 12 contains perhaps the clearest witness to the reality of resurrection anywhere in the Old Testament. "And many of those who sleep in the dust of the earth shall awake, some to everlasting life, and some to shame and everlasting contempt" (12:2). This is a stunning message of hope for the beleaguered Old Testament believers to whom Daniel writes; it is not unlike the promise Jesus gives in John 5: "Truly, truly, I say to you, an hour is coming, and is now here, when the dead will hear the voice of the Son of God, and those who hear will live" (John 5:25). But, as we see in Daniel, Jesus goes on to clarify that this resurrection will actually be a *double resurrection*, a resurrection that issues in both blessing and judgment: "those who have done good to the resurrection of life, and those who have done evil to the resurrection of judgment" (John 5:29). For those who die in Christ, a glorious resurrection awaits (see 1 Cor. 15:50–56); for those who die in unbelief, there is only judgment.

▶ Personal Implications

Take time to reflect on the implications of Daniel 10:1–12:13 for your own life today. Consider what you have learned that might lead you to praise God, repent of sin, and trust in his gracious promises. Make notes below on the personal implications for your walk with the Lord of the (1) *Gospel Glimpses*, (2) *Whole-Bible Connections*, (3) *Theological Soundings*, and (4) this passage as a whole.

1. Gospel Glimpses

2. Whole-Bible Connections

3. Theological Soundings

4. Daniel 10:1–12:13

As You Finish This Unit . . .

Take a moment now to ask for the Lord's blessing and help as you continue in this study of Daniel. And take a moment also to look back through this unit of study, to reflect on some key things that the Lord may be teaching you—and perhaps to highlight and underline these things to review again in the future.

Definitions

[1] **Predestine/predestination** – God's sovereign choice of people for redemption and eternal life. Also referred to as "election."

[2] **Demon** – An evil spirit that can inhabit a human being and influence him or her to carry out its will. Demons (fallen and corrupted angels) were created by God and are always limited by God. Jesus and his followers cast out many demons, demonstrating Jesus' superiority over them. All demons will one day be destroyed along with Satan (Matt. 25:41; Rev. 20:10).

Week 12: Summary and Conclusion

We will conclude our study of Daniel by summarizing the big picture of God's message through Daniel as a whole. Then we will consider several questions in order to reflect on various Gospel Glimpses, Whole-Bible Connections, and Theological Soundings throughout the entire book.

The Big Picture of Daniel

Daniel is a fascinating book, for many reasons. The opening six chapters contain some of the most dramatic and exciting narratives in the Bible. We also grow to admire the conviction and courage of Daniel and his three friends, as their faith is tested and put on display, so to speak, again and again in those opening chapters. There is much to be gleaned by attending closely to the lives of these great saints of old.

But Daniel also intrigues us because of its visions, and the sheer scope of what it covers. Not only do we gain insight into Israel's own history, from exile to return, but we are also given a sweeping view of human history, from the rise of the Babylonian empire to the conquest and ultimate destruction of the Roman empire many centuries later. Daniel is thus a masterful blend of sacred and secular history; in fact, what we see is that these two histories are one, being closely intertwined by God's own design.

Furthermore, Daniel opens our eyes to the fact that there is always more going on than meets the eye. What we can gather with our five senses is not the whole story; indeed, it may be only a reflection of a more important story—a cosmic battle taking place in the heavenly realms, which we cannot see with our human eyes, but only with the eyes of faith.

Ultimately, however, the book of Daniel is about God—his character, his plans, his purpose for the world. God is the main actor in Daniel, as he is everywhere in the Bible. And while we often have reason to be worried, if not discouraged, by the appearance of things all around us in our fallen and sin-wracked world, the book of Daniel serves as a powerful reminder that God is on his throne and is sure to get his victory. What is more, one day God will put the world to rights, destroying unrighteousness and ushering in his eternal kingdom.

▶ Gospel Glimpses

The whole premise of the book of Daniel is that Israel has failed to keep the terms of the Sinai covenant and thus has come under God's judgment and has been sent into exile. And yet the whole message of the book of Daniel is that God is not only merciful to forgive but also powerful to effect restoration and even return for his people. Even though the people of God may suffer in this life, they can bank on the fact that God will not abandon them but will one day achieve his victory in the world and in their lives. This, of course, is the message of the gospel itself, as it is revealed to us in the person and work of Jesus Christ. "For all have sinned and fall short of the glory of God," Scripture says (Rom. 3:23), but God has provided a way to be right with him, "through the redemption that is in Christ Jesus" (v. 24). And although we continue to endure suffering, we can rest confidently in our future victory in God and thus "rejoice in hope of the glory of God" (Rom. 5:2).

Has Daniel brought new clarity to your understanding of the gospel? How so?

Were there any particular passages or themes in Daniel that led you to a fresh understanding and grasp of God's grace to us through Jesus?

▶ Whole-Bible Connections

Perhaps no other book of the Old Testament is as formative of the eschatology of the New Testament authors, and of Jesus himself, as is the book of Daniel. In it we are given a sweeping view of redemptive history, from the time of the exile to the time of Christ and beyond. We're also given a powerful picture of how the Abrahamic blessing unfolds through the lives of God's people, in this case Daniel and his three friends, into the lives of the nations, from Nebuchadnezzar the Babylonian to Darius the Mede.

How has this study of Daniel filled out your understanding of the biblical storyline of redemption?

Were there any themes emphasized in Daniel that help you to deepen your grasp of the Bible's unity?

Have any passages or themes expanded your understanding of the redemption that Jesus provides, which he began at his first coming and will consummate at his return?

What connections between Daniel and the New Testament were new to you?

Theological Soundings

Daniel has much to contribute to Christian theology. Numerous doctrines and themes are developed, clarified, and reinforced throughout Daniel, especially the sovereignty of God, the relationship of church and state, and the eschatological kingdom of God.

Has your theology shifted in minor or major ways during the course of studying Daniel? How so?

How has your understanding of the nature and character of God been deepened throughout this study?

What unique contributions does Daniel make toward our understanding of who Jesus is and what he accomplished through his life, death, and resurrection?

What, specifically, does Daniel teach us about the human condition and our need of redemption?

Personal Implications

God wrote the book of Daniel to transform us. As you reflect on Daniel as a whole, what implications do you see for your life?

What implications for life flow from your reflections on the questions already asked in this week's study concerning Gospel Glimpses, Whole-Bible Connections, and Theological Soundings?

What have you learned in Daniel that might lead you to praise God, turn away from sin, or trust more firmly in his promises?

▶ As You Finish Studying Daniel . . .

We rejoice with you as you finish studying the book of Daniel! May this study become part of your Christian walk of faith, day by day and week by week throughout all your life. Now we would greatly encourage you to study the Word of God on a week-by-week basis. To continue your study of the Bible, we would encourage you to consider other books in the *Knowing the Bible* series, and to visit www.knowingthebibleseries.org.

Lastly, take a moment to look back through this study. Review the notes that you have written, and the things that you have highlighted or underlined. Reflect again on the key themes that the Lord has been teaching you about himself and about his Word. May these things become a treasure for you throughout your life—this we pray in the name of the Father, and the Son, and the Holy Spirit. Amen.

KNOWING THE BIBLE STUDY GUIDE SERIES

Experience the *Grace* of God in the *Word* of God, Book by Book

—— Series Volumes ——

- Genesis
- Exodus
- Leviticus
- Numbers
- Deuteronomy
- Joshua
- Judges
- Ruth and Esther
- 1–2 Samuel
- 1–2 Kings
- 1–2 Chronicles
- Ezra and Nehemiah
- Job
- Psalms
- Proverbs
- Ecclesiastes
- Song of Solomon

- Isaiah
- Jeremiah
- Lamentations, Habakkuk, and Zephaniah
- Ezekiel
- Daniel
- Hosea
- Joel, Amos, and Obadiah
- Jonah, Micah, and Nahum
- Haggai, Zechariah, and Malachi
- Matthew
- Mark
- Luke

- John
- Acts
- Romans
- 1 Corinthians
- 2 Corinthians
- Galatians
- Ephesians
- Philippians
- Colossians and Philemon
- 1–2 Thessalonians
- 1–2 Timothy and Titus
- Hebrews
- James
- 1–2 Peter and Jude
- 1–3 John
- Revelation

crossway.org/knowingthebible